52 Weeks of Wisdom

A Woman's Guide To Self-Empowerment

VOLUME 1

Susan L. Farrell, MBA

SLF PUBLISHING • LEBANON, WI

Copyright ©2015 Susan L. Farrell. All Rights Reserved.

No part of this book may be reproduced or transmitted in any form or by any means, electronic or mechanical, including photocopying, recording, or by any information storage and retrieval system, without written permission of the author, except for the inclusion of brief quotations in a review. For permission, contact the author at **info@susanlfarrell.com**.

ISBN: 978-0-9889090-1-4

First Edition

Published by SLF Publishing, P.O. Box 172, Lebanon, WI 53047

Cover and interior design by AbandonedWest Creative, Inc.

IMPORTANT DISCLAIMER

The purpose of this book is to encourage the reader to think about her or his actions and to make changes if she or he wants to do so. It is based primarily upon the author's experiences. It is not intended to give advice. The author and SLF Publishing shall have neither liability nor responsibility to any person or entity with respect to any loss or damage caused, or alleged to have been caused, directly or indirectly, by the information contained in this book. If you do not wish to be bound by the above, you may return this book to the publisher for a full refund.

This book is dedicated to my immediate and extended family.
Thank you for your phenomenal influence!

Contents

Foreword 9
Introduction 11
1 Self-Empowerment 13
2 Mental Health Days 15
3 You Can Lead A Horse To Water... 17
4 Rip Off the Bandage 19
5 No Reality, Only Perception 21
6 Rights And Responsibilities 23
7 Write Your Epitaph 25
8 Do You Make Things Happen,
   or Do You Wait For Things To Happen? 27
9 Feelings, Rights, and Responsibilities 29
10 Root Cause Analysis 31
11 Finish What You Start 33
12 Do What is Right, but Right for Whom? 35
13 Try! 37
14 Achieving Your Goals 39
15 Play Your Own Game 41
16 Great Success Requires Great Risk 43
17 Stop Digging 45
18 We Always Have Choices 47
19 Pay Now or Pay Later 49
20 What is Your ROTI? 51
21 20/20 Hindsight 53
22 Aim Accurately 55
23 Be Tolerant 57

24	Be *Your* Best	59
25	Big Dreams, Small Dreams	61
26	Bits and Pieces	63
27	Business or Hobby?	65
28	Hard Work Works	67
29	Just Do Something	69
30	Lessons From *Mary Poppins*	71
31	Values	73
32	Who We Are	75
33	Do Things that Make You Smile	77
34	Easer or Jumper?	79
35	Persistence or Stubbornness?	81
36	Stop Complaining and Do Something	83
37	Embrace Yourself While Improving Yourself	85
38	Use It or Lose It	87
39	The Success We Think We Deserve	89
40	Study for A's?	91
41	Stop Studying and Start Doing	93
42	Routines	95
43	Business, Hobby, or Required Responsibility?	97
44	Clean House or Change Oil?	99
45	Battling Boxes	101
46	Be Sensitive, but…	103
47	Worry, Friend or Foe?	105
48	Dress to Connect	107
49	No Magic Pill	109
50	Keep Your Word	111
51	Time Wasters	113
52	Equal Partnerships	115
	Conclusion	117
	Author's Note	119
	Acknowledgments	121
	About the Author	123

What do you do?
Why do you do it?
Do you want to change?

You have the power within you to become the person you want and to create the life you desire.

Self-empowerment is giving yourself permission and taking responsibility to achieve it.

Foreword

Every time I read one of Susan's posts or watch her video my reaction is, "Yes! How did she know I needed this now?" Invariably, she causes me to stop and think about the way I am running my business and my life. Her post in June titled "The Success We Think We Deserve" about self-sabotage and success is posted on my wall. I reread it every Monday as part of my weekly planning ritual as a reminder to myself to take charge and stay out of my own way. Susan has a way of shining a light on the ignored and forgotten strengths, weaknesses, and values that drive us and make us special.

Sue Gresham
LinkedIn Coach, Trainer and Social Media Strategist
Owner of Innovative Client Solutions

Introduction

There are many ways to read this book.

I suggest that you read one topic per week. Pick a day when you can read it and think about what it means to you. If you can pick the same day each week, perhaps Friday morning, it can become a habit and easier to remember to do.

At the end of each topic is space to write notes to yourself. You might want to write what this topic means to you. More importantly, you might want to write any changes that you want to make based upon the insights you have gained.

Of course, you can read the entire book in one sitting; it is your choice.

However you decide to use this book, I hope it will give you additional insights on not just what you do, but why you do it, so that you can make the changes necessary to create the life you want.

Self-Empowerment 1

Empowerment is external, self-empowerment is internal.

Empowerment is when someone has power, permission, and/or authority to do something. This often comes from outside the person. For example, our supervisor might empower us to make decisions related to the business. We might empower our attorney to make legal decisions for us. Laws might empower women to have more equal status in the workplace.

Self-empowerment comes from inside of us. It is when we give ourselves the power, permission, and/or authority to do something. This might be to grow and develop into the person we want. It might be to create the life we want. We have the power within us to create what we desire. Often what stands in our way is that we do not think we have the right to it. We need to give ourselves permission to go after what we want.

1

Self-empowerment is when we use our power to take control of all aspects of our life. It is when we take responsibility for our choices, our thoughts, our actions and the consequences of these. It is when we decide what we want, develop a plan on how to achieve it, and implement the plan.

This applies to our professional and personal life. Each impacts the other. An important benefit to this is that the knowledge and skills that make you successful in one aspect of your life can assist in another. For example, skills that you learn to deal with less-than-desirable co-workers can often be used to deal with pesky relatives who refuse to fall off the family tree.

To take control of your life it is important to be aware of what makes you *you*. What are your thoughts? Values? Beliefs? Passions? Goals? Motivations? Who are you, and why are you the way you are? This helps you determine why you do the things you do.

My writing is designed to provide you with opportunities to think about various topics. From this you might gain a new perspective about yourself, your thoughts and beliefs, your motivations, and your actions. After that, it becomes easier to make changes in your thoughts and behaviors, if you decide to do so.

Notes

Mental Health Days 2

Sometimes we need to take a "mental health day."

We might not be sick. There might not be anything physically wrong with us. But we just do not feel right and need to take a little time for ourselves.

This has happened to me. As an example, one day I was feeling really irritable. I could not focus. I was not accomplishing anything. I was getting really frustrated. Finally about mid-morning I told myself enough was enough and I was taking a mental health day.

I left my home office, treated myself to a mid-morning snack at a local bakery, ran some errands, and took care of a few things for myself. In the process, I ran into my brother, who was in town to see a client. We had a nice chat. I treated myself to a late lunch. (I like eating out.)

2

It was one of the first really nice days of the spring season, perfect for putting the top down on the car. When I returned home, I found reasons to go driving again just to enjoy the weather. When I returned home again, I spent some time reading.

The next day I felt great! I was energetic and enthusiastic. I was so productive that I more than made up for taking the previous day off. Taking a day off was what I needed. I needed a mental health day.

Being self-employed has its advantages. As long as I meet deadlines, it does not matter if I work at noon or at midnight. This makes it easier for me to take a day off than if I punched a time clock.

If you can—and if you will not negatively affect other people—when you know you really need to take a day off, take a mental health day. You will feel so much better the next day.

Notes

You Can Lead a Horse to Water... **3**

We have all heard the phrase, "You can lead a horse to water, but you can't make it drink."

There are two points I would like to make about this statement.

If you are the handler, you cannot make the horse drink. You can lead it to water and do everything to encourage the horse to drink, but you cannot force it to do so. In the same way, you can provide information, education, resources, assistance, and encouragement to others, but you cannot make them learn and you cannot make them change. It must be their decision to learn and change.

There may come a time when you need to decide that it is not worth trying to get someone to "drink" any longer. You may decide that your time and effort are better spent where they will make a difference. This may occur in both your professional and personal life.

3 Look at it from a different perspective. What do you do if you are the "horse"? If someone leads you to water, do you drink? If someone offers you information, education, resources, assistance, or encouragement, do you learn and change? Or do you refuse? Why?

If you can determine the real reasons you do not want to learn and change when given the opportunity, you may discover hurdles that are reining you in from achieving the professional and personal success that you desire.

Notes

Rip Off the Bandage 4

When I was a child and got hurt, Mom would clean the wound, put on antibiotic, and put a bandage on the wound.

When the time came to take the bandage off, I never wanted to do it. I knew it would hurt. So I would try to take it off slowly and carefully. It would still hurt a little, and it would continue to hurt for as long as it took me to take off the bandage. I could prolong this process for a very long time.

Dad would say, "Just rip it off. Get it over with." I finally tried it. It hurt! But it did not hurt for long. It certainly did not hurt for as long as it did when I slowly tried to peel it off. If there was a way to measure the acuity and duration of pain for both processes, it would probably show that there was less pain with ripping it off.

In life, we will always be faced with painful situations, painful decisions. We can delay making a decision, delay taking action. Or we can "rip off the bandage" and get it done. Although it may be more painful at the moment, there will probably be less total pain than if we delay taking action.

Do you have any "bandages" that you have been slowly trying to remove? Do you have relationships that need to be addressed, or maybe ended? Do you have a job that you need to leave? Would it be better if you just "ripped off the bandage," faced the pain, and moved on?

Notes

No Reality, Only Perception

5

We have all heard the phrase, "There is no reality, only perception." The world is to each of us what we perceive it to be.

Some people perceive the world to be wonderful, and others perceive it to be horrendous. How we perceive our lives becomes our reality. How we perceive *ourselves* becomes our reality.

To me, it seems that there are three types of people when it comes to self-perception.

There are those who do not give themselves enough credit. They do not think they are that good or that worthy. They focus on their failures. If this sounds like you, try focusing on your strengths and talents. You may be a much better person, and much better at what you do, than you think.

There are also those who create a perception about themselves that is much better than what others have of them. They may do this to make themselves feel good about

5 themselves, to justify past actions, or to avoid looking too closely at who they really are. If this might be you, consider being honest with yourself. If there are things in your life that you want to improve, you cannot make good decisions with faulty information.

And then there are those individuals who have a pretty accurate perception of themselves. They see their faults and work to overcome them rather than let the faults define who they are. They see their strengths and accomplishments and take credit for their hard work and persistence. If this is you, congratulations!

Which type do you think you are? Are there any changes you would like to make in your perception of yourself?

Notes

Rights and Responsibilities 6

We all have rights. With these rights, however, come responsibilities.

For example, we have the right to our opinion. We have the right to voice our opinion. Remember the First Amendment? Freedom of Speech? We legally have this right. We also have the responsibility to voice our opinion while respecting others. For example, if we state what we think of someone's actions, that is better than attacking the person and calling names. Also, keep in mind that others have a right to voice their opinions and have different opinions than we do.

We have the right to the professional life we want. With that comes the responsibility for gaining the knowledge and skills to enter that profession or career. We are responsible for gaining knowledge and skills as necessary. If we want to be promoted, we are responsible for working to the level necessary to advance.

6

We have the right to the personal life we want, provided that we do not harm others. We are responsible for creating the personal life we want. If we want positive relationships with people, we need to work at them. Great relationships do not just happen. Of course, the other person needs to take responsibility as well. If he/she does not, maybe the relationship is not worth maintaining. Remember that something as simple as happiness is our responsibility. It is not anyone else's responsibility to make us happy.

If we want a house, car, land, vacations, and all the other things that money can buy, we are responsible for earning the money to purchase them. No one else is responsible for giving us what we want. If we are not willing to work for it ourselves, why should anyone else want to make sacrifices to give it to us?

When we accept responsibility for our decisions, actions, and lives, then we can truly accept the rights we have. Are you taking full advantage of your rights by taking full responsibility for your life?

Notes

Write Your Epitaph   7

An exercise to help in goal setting is to write your own obituary.

When you pass away at age 80, 90, 100, or whatever you desire, what do you want your obituary to say? What accomplishments do you want to have recorded? What do you want people to say about you?

This can help you determine what your life goals are. Once you know what your goals are, you can develop and implement a plan to achieve them.

A similar exercise, and one that may require more thought, is to write your epitaph. What one sentence do you want on your grave marker to sum up who you were? This can be difficult to do because of the limited number of words. It becomes necessary to distill your essence. This describes you as a person, not necessarily your accomplishments.

7

I think this may be what I will want: "Susan was a wise woman of integrity." I am not wise yet, although I do well with the integrity part. I may change my mind, but for now I think striving for this is worthwhile.

What do you want as your epitaph?

Notes

Do You Make Things Happen, or Do You Wait for Things to Happen?

People who make things happen know what they want.

They develop a plan to make it happen; they implement the plan; and they regularly evaluate their results. If they are achieving the results they want, great. If not, they reevaluate their plan, revise it as necessary, and implement the new plan. They do this continuously. Because of this, they make things happen. They create the life they desire.

People who make things happen go after life. They go after what they want. They also take full and complete responsibility for their life.

Other people may go through the motions of developing and implementing plans, but mostly they are waiting for things to happen. They are waiting for someone else to do things for them, provide for them, care for them. They are waiting for that perfect job or relationship to magically appear. They are waiting for life to come to them.

Which type of person are you? Do you make things happen? Or do you wait for things to happen?

I am proud to say that I am someone who makes things happen. If you are too, great! If you are not, I suggest that you decide to become someone who makes things happen. Life, personally and professionally, is much fuller and more satisfying when you make the life you want rather than wait for it to magically appear. Even at Hogwarts, magic did not just happen. Someone had to make it happen by waving a wand, incanting a spell, or stirring a potion.

Take control of your life, and make things happen.

Notes

Feelings, Rights, and Responsibilities   9

We have the right to feel everything that we do.

Along with that right is the responsibility to express these feelings appropriately.

We have the right to feel all the positive emotions: happiness, joy, excitement, accomplishment, and love, among others. We also have the right to feel all the so-called negative emotions such as anger, hurt, despair, and grief.

I do not like the term negative emotions. All of these emotions are just part of life. I think we all go through them at some point in our lives. If we do not, then maybe we have a problem feeling what we are meant to feel. We cannot let these emotions control our lives, however. We need to accept them, address them, and move on.

Along with the right to feel all these emotions are responsibilities. We have the right to feel anything and

9

everything we do. We also have the responsibility to express these feelings appropriately.

For example, we have the right to feel angry when someone does something to hurt us. We have the right to tell that person how what he or she did affected us. The responsibility comes in with how we tell him or her. If we tell the person, with respect, what we feel and why, that is good. We do not have the right to treat the person disrespectfully. We do not have the right to yell at the person or call names. We certainly do not have the right to physically harm the person.

What is considered appropriate depends upon the situation. If we want to cry our eyes out at home, that is fine, as long as we do not scare the children or the pets. It is not appropriate to do that in the workplace, however.

What is considered appropriate also depends upon the person. What we say to an adult is different than what we say to a child, for example. What we say to a stranger might be different than what we say to a friend.

Do not deny your feelings. Do not stuff them deep inside of you and hope they will go away. They will not. They will just fester inside you like an infection. Before you express these feelings, however, think of the most appropriate way to do so under the circumstances.

Notes

Root Cause Analysis 10

In medicine, it is critical that an accurate diagnosis be made so that the disease can be treated, and not just the symptoms.

For example, if you go to a doctor with stomach pains and she simply gives you something to make the pain go away, it will not do you any good if you have cancer. The cancer needs to be treated, not just the pain.

Also, the best treatment depends upon the disease. The treatment would be different if you had an ulcer than if you had cancer. An accurate diagnosis is critical.

In business, root cause analysis is often used to determine why something went wrong. In essence, the process involves determining what happened, why it happened, and how to prevent it from happening again. Of course, the same process can be used when good things happen. Determine what happened, why it happened, and how to repeat the positive results.

10

Root cause analysis is very similar to making an accurate diagnosis.

These same concepts can be used in our personal and professional lives. If we define what happened and determine why, we can develop a plan to achieve the results we want. The critical aspect is determining why.

It does not matter whether you want to consider this process as diagnosing what is happening in your life or as root cause analysis. The important thing is that you do analyze what is happening and why. You may need to ask yourself, "And why else?" multiple times before you get a complete answer. Once you do have a complete answer, act on the information.

You cannot make good decisions with bad or incomplete information. Make sure your analysis is complete and that you have all the "whys" before developing a plan to address them.

This can be a painful process as it may show that we have weaknesses that we do not want to admit. But it is necessary to achieve the success we want.

Notes

Finish What You Start 11

For me, starting projects is easy. New projects are fun and exciting. The difficulty is finishing them.

Finishing is what matters, however. It is in finishing the project that we get the results we want.

There are many reasons we do not finish what we start. We get busy, we get tired, or other things demand our time. Sometimes we do not finish out of fear because if we do finish, things may change. Sometimes we do not finish because we did not create and implement a plan to make the change happen.

Often we do not finish because we did not make a commitment. Talk is not enough. We have to take action. And usually we have to take action over and over again.

I have a friend who told me for 15 years that her boss was horrible and that she had to find a new job. For 15 years I agreed with her. Although she took a few forays into the

11

job market during that time, it took her 15 years to finally commit to finding a new job. Once she did commit, she found a much better job.

I have another friend who 20 years ago decided he wanted to be a writer. He has never finished a manuscript. Since he has not finished one, he has never had one to sell. He has never really made the commitment to investing the time and energy it takes to be successful as a writer.

I have many friends who have been very successful in new careers, new business ventures, and even new lives. I admire them greatly. I do not think that, in general, they are any smarter than my other two friends. I also do not think they have any more luck. What they do have is the commitment to finish what they start, no matter what happens.

Do you finish what you start? Do you finish it timely?

Notes

Do What is Right, but Right for Whom? 12

Generally, a good rule of thumb is to do what is right. Not necessarily what is easy, or what we want, but what is right.

Suppose what is right for another is not right for us, however. If it is something that will harm us, then the answer is easy—do not do it.

What if it will not harm us but is not convenient for us? Or it will not hurt us, but we really do not feel like doing it? Then the answer is much more difficult. On the one hand, we need to take care of ourselves. On the other, we have responsibilities to others, especially to those who depend upon us.

I do not think there are any easy answers to this. It depends upon the situation and the participants. These are the guidelines I try to use:

- Is it my sole responsibility to do it? If yes, then I do it.
- Is it primarily my responsibility to do it? If yes, then I do it

unless there is someone else responsible, available, and willing to do it.
- Is it something that needs to be done, and am I the most capable, available, and/or qualified to do it? If yes, then I generally do it.
- Is it something that is someone else's responsibility? If yes, then I may do it if the person does not ask for help often. If the person is capable of doing it herself and yet frequently asks for help, I usually say no. There comes a point in time when I do not want someone to take advantage of me and I do not want to enable that person not to take responsibility.
- If I do not do it, will someone come to harm regardless of whose responsibility it is? If yes, then I do it if I can.

Determining the right thing to do can be a difficult balancing act. If we at least think about it first and make a conscious decision, we will probably make a good decision.

Notes

Try! 13

I am not an avid baseball fan, but I do know a little about the game. Something that fascinates me is that if a player has a batting average of .300 it is considered good.

This means that the player succeeds (gets a hit) 30% of the time and fails 70% of the time.

How many of us consider ourselves failures if we are not "batting" .500? .900? How many of us consider ourselves failures if we do not hit a home run every time we go to bat?

Sometimes I think we are too hard on ourselves and need to step back and put things into perspective. We are not going to hit a home run every time. We are not even going to get a hit every time.

But if we continue to go to the plate and try our best, we will do better than those sitting on the bench. At least at the plate we have a possibility of getting a hit, and maybe a home run. We do not have any chance as long as we sit on the bench.

13 Give yourself credit for going to the plate and trying. You are automatically more successful than those who continue to sit on the bench.

Notes

Achieving Your Goals 14

There is so much that can be written about setting and achieving goals. What I would like to do today is to try to simplify goal achievement.

Our goals really revolve around the following:

- What do we want to do?
- Where do we want to go?
- Who do we want to be?

We answer these questions. These are our goals.

Our action plan describes how we are going to achieve these goals.

Both steps are relatively easy. The difficulty is in implementing the plan. Successful implementation requires that we ask ourselves throughout the day whether our actions will help us reach our goals. If yes, then continue with the action. If no, then do not.

14

As a very simple example, pretend that your goal is to go on vacation. You have determined where you want to go and how much it will cost. Later, you are shopping and see a pair of shoes you really like, but do not need. Will buying the shoes help you reach your goal of saving money to go on vacation? No. So do not buy the shoes.

As another example, pretend that your goal is to get a promotion at work. You have a project that is due Monday. You can work over the weekend and complete it or tell your supervisor it will not be ready on Monday and ask for an extension. Which decision will help you reach your goal of a promotion?

Our goal achievement is based on all the little decisions we make each day. Are you making decisions that will help you reach your goals?

Notes

Play Your Own Game 15

There is a great deal of pressure for us to measure ourselves and our success by what others do.

To a certain extent, this can be good. It can help us strive and achieve more of what we want.

Sometimes, though, it can be detrimental. We might not want what others want. We might not want to make the sacrifices necessary to achieve that level of success. We might not have the knowledge, skills, and talent that others have, and it might not be realistic to try to obtain them.

If we measure ourselves against others, we may not appreciate that the total life we have is what we really want.

This occurred to me when my husband and I were playing golf. His golf game goals are different than mine. He wants to consistently shoot below 90. I want to enjoy being outside, getting some exercise, and shooting a better average score this year than last year. If I try to play his golf game, or if he tries

15 to play mine, neither of us will be happy. As long as we keep in mind what our individual goals are, we both have fun.

In your professional and personal life, play your own game. Play the game that makes you happy, and do not worry about the game others are playing.

Notes

Great Success Requires Great Risk

Risk comes in many forms.

Sometimes it is financial risk such as leaving a well paying job to become self-employed. Sometimes it is a time risk such as investing the time in an education or new venture which takes time away from family. Sometimes it is a relationship risk by saying something to someone about an issue that bothers you.

If we never take risks, however, we will never move beyond where we are. Everyone has a different comfort level for risk. This is understandable. It is also important to understand, however, that if we take only small risks, we will achieve only small successes. If this is acceptable to you, then there is no problem. If you want great success, however, the only way to achieve it is to take great risks.

16

Taking a risk is, of course, risky. If we take a big risk we may achieve big success. Or we may fail and lose big. If we take small risks and fail, then we only lose small.

There is no right or wrong. If your comfort level for risk is low and you do not want to take big risks because you do not want the possibility of big losses, that is your decision. But then accept that one reason you do not have big success is that you are not willing to take big risks.

Again, there is no right or wrong. Only you can decide what is right for you. Just accept responsibility for the consequences of your decisions.

Notes

Stop Digging 17

One of my father's favorite sayings was, "If you find that you have dug yourself into a hole, the very first thing you have to do is stop digging."

We all get ourselves into trouble sometimes. It may be in our professional or personal lives. It may be in big ways or small. It happens to all of us.

When we realize we have dug ourselves into a hole, we need to determine what we did that got us into that situation and then stop doing it. It sounds so simple, and yet it can be very difficult. If forces us to honestly look at ourselves and our actions. It then forces us to evaluate what we did, why, and make corrections.

Self-evaluation and change are difficult. If we do not do this, however, we will find that we will never get out of the hole that we have dug for ourselves.

17 **Notes**

We Always Have Choices 18

In any situation, we have choices— emphasis on the plural.

It bothers me when someone says that she did something because she did not have a choice. Wrong! At a minimum, there are always two choices. Do something, or do nothing.

There are always choices. There might be only one good choice out of a dozen bad choices, but there are still choices. Even deciding to do something rather than nothing is a choice. Deciding not to decide is still making a choice.

When we tell ourselves that we did something because we did not have a choice, it is a negative. It is giving away our power. When we take ownership of the choice we made, it is a positive. It reaffirms that we have control over our lives. If we pick the one good choice out of a dozen bad choices, we need to take credit for it.

Can you see all the choices possible in your situations?

18 Notes

Pay Now or Pay Later 19

**Everything in life has a price.
It may be a price in money, time,
or other intangibles.**

Once we spend money on one item, we do not have that money to spend on another item. Once we spend time on one activity, we do not have that time to spend on any other activity.

If we buy on credit, not only do we pay the initial price, but we also pay interest. What "interest" are we paying when we put off doing the things that will create the success we want in our personal and professional lives?

For example, if you are putting off going back to school, what is it costing you, year after year, in lost income and potential opportunities? You will still pay the same in money (or more) and the same in time, but the longer you wait the less time you will have to reap the rewards.

What will you pay in the future by not looking for a new job now? What will it cost you to continue to delay it? What will it cost you to continue to sit in front of the TV instead of spending quality time with your family?

We will always pay for what we get. We can pay later, and gain less. Or we can pay now, and have longer to gain from it, thus gaining more.

Notes

What is Your ROTI? 20

Return on investment (ROI) is used in business frequently to evaluate the profitability of a decision. Will the return be worth the investment?

This is something that can be used in our personal lives as well. For example, what will our ROI be on a purchase we make?

Something else to consider is our ROTI—return on time investment. (I do not think this is a real business term. But it is a good concept.)

Is what we are doing giving us a good return? We all have the same minutes in each day. Are we spending our time wisely? Are we making the most of our time? Are we spending our time in such a way that we will meet our professional and personal goals?

We are all busy. ROTI is something that can help us prioritize how to spend our time. If we ask, "What return will I get on the time I invest doing this?" it may help us make better decisions.

20 Notes

20/20 Hindsight **21**

Do you use your 20/20 hindsight?

Our vision of what we should have done is usually 20/20. Because we know what we did and what happened because of it, we know what we should have done.

We cannot change what has already happened. However, how often do we use the lessons we learned when similar situations occur?

If we apply what we learned from 20/20 hindsight, we can greatly improve our vision of current situations. Better vision leads to better decisions.

21 Notes

Aim Accurately 22

Do you aim for your goals?
Are you sure?

A problem that I have in golf is aiming. Whenever I think that I am aiming at the pin, the ball goes to the right. Consistently. When I aim to the left of the pin, the ball goes straight for the pin.

As I thought about this, I realized that this could happen in our professional and personal lives as well. We may think we are aiming for our goals. However, if we consistently miss our goals, then something is wrong.

Remember: there is no reality, only perception. Our perception may be that we are aiming for our goals, but if the reality is that we are missing our goals, our aim may be off.

The most common correction is to change how or where we are aiming.

22

When I change how I am aiming for the pin, the ball goes toward the pin. I have found that this is also true in life. There are times when no matter how hard I try, I cannot reach a goal. When I stop and analyze the situation, and adjust my aim, often I can then reach the goal.

If you are not meeting a professional or personal goal, stop and analyze how and where you are aiming. You may have better success if you modify your aim. Where you think you are aiming may not be where you are actually aiming. It is the reality and perception concept.

Notes

Be Tolerant 23

It is easy to get frustrated with people. They do not always think the way you do or do things the way you would.

First, that does not mean that they are wrong. Rarely is there only one way. What you do works for you. Maybe what they do works for them without hurting anyone else.

Second, maybe they are learning and trying something that is new to them. There is a learning curve. Someday they may be as good as, or better than, you.

As long as the other person is not doing you any harm, be tolerant.

Notes

Be *Your* Best 24

To succeed in our professional and personal lives it is important to strive to be our best every day.

Realistically, some days we will do better than other days. As long as we continue to strive to do our best, however, we will continue to improve. This means that our "best" will continue to move upward.

The key is that we strive to do *our* best, not someone else's best. There will always be someone who is smarter than we are, more successful than we are, and has more than we have. That does not matter. What matters is that we improve and be the best we can.

Sometimes we may find ourselves in the opposite situation, however; maybe we are the best in our group. Our true friends will be happy for us and support us in becoming even better.

Others, though, might be jealous and try to bring us down

24 to their level. Some people can build themselves up only by tearing others down. Do not let them do this to you.

Always strive to be your best, even if it makes you much more successful than the others around you. Always try to improve.

When we can see improvement in ourselves, it gives us more confidence. With additional confidence, we can do even better. Always strive to be *your* best.

Notes

Big Dreams, Small Dreams **25**

Which do you think are more important, big dreams or small dreams? I think what is most important are those dreams that become reality.

Small dreams accomplished are better than big dreams never realized.

It is important to our professional and personal success to dream. If we do not, we will never get what we want.

There are many people who say that we should never, ever, give up on our dreams. I am too pragmatic to believe that. There comes a time when we have to look at our dreams and determine whether they are achievable. We may not have, nor can we obtain, the abilities, skills, or knowledge to achieve our big dreams. We may not have the time, money, ability, or dedication to achieve our big dreams, or at least we may not want to put those resources toward it. We may not be willing to pay the price to achieve our dreams.

As long as we continue to pursue a dream, this is time,

money, and energy that we do not have to pursue anything else.

For example, I would love to be a science fiction writer like Anne McCaffrey. I am in awe of the worlds she created and the inspiration she was to others, especially women.

After many attempts, I know that I do not have the ability to write entertaining, engaging fiction. That does not mean, however, that I cannot be an author. I am. One of my most satisfying accomplishments was writing and self-publishing, *Don't Act Like Prey! A Guide to Self-Empowerment for Women*. You are reading my second book, and there are more books in the works.

I may not have accomplished a big dream of being a world-renowned science fiction author, but I have accomplished a small dream of being an author and helping people.

Look at your dreams and the length of time you have spent on them. Are you any closer to achieving them than you were 5 years ago? 10? 20? If not, it may be time to honestly evaluate your dreams and the real reasons you have not achieved them. Are they dreams, or daydreams?

Perhaps you have not worked hard enough or smart enough to achieve them. Or perhaps it is time to redefine them.

Notes

Bits and Pieces 26

An old management adage is, "How do you eat an elephant? One bite at a time."

All this refers to is that you take something large and complex, such as a project, and break it down into smaller, more manageable pieces. By breaking it down into smaller pieces, it is not as formidable and is easier to accomplish.

I have done this successfully for years in business. I rarely have enough time to complete a project all at once. However, by working on one section at a time, I finish the project. In addition, it is completed more quickly than if I had waited until I had enough time to complete it all at once.

Another example is education. Few adults have the luxury of going back to school full time. I did not. However, by taking one class per semester, in a few years I completed my MBA. If I had waited until I could devote full time to it, I would still be waiting.

26

I have discovered that this concept works just as well for personal projects. For example, I had wanted to clean out and rearrange my kitchen cupboards and pantry for a couple of years. Finally, I just started doing one cupboard or shelf when I had 15-20 minutes. This usually occurred while I cooked dinner. Within a few weeks, I had accomplished more than in the previous two years.

Are there projects, personal or professional, that you have wanted to do for some time and have not completed? Would it help to do them "one bite at a time?"

Notes

Business or Hobby? 27

"Businesses are in business to make money. If it does not make money, it is not a business. It is a hobby."

This was the most valuable piece of information I learned when I went to the University of Louisville for an MBA. (If I could remember the professor's name, I would give him the credit. Unfortunately, I do not even remember the class.)

This forced me to take a very critical look at my business at the time. I have used it to evaluate my business many times since.

If you are self-employed, do you treat your business as a business? Or do you treat it as hobby? Do you invest as much time in your business as you would if you were punching a time clock? Or do you fit in time when you can in between personal pursuits?

I know people who run their businesses as a business. They

27

put in the time and effort needed to achieve the success they want.

I know others who consistently let everything else come first. It can be easy to do, especially if you work from home. There are many potential distractions.

The ones who are most successful are those who treat it as a business. They work extremely long, hard hours. If you want a business, that is the price to pay.

If what you really want is a hobby, that is fine if you have another way to support yourself. But at least be honest with yourself. A simple question to ask yourself is whether or not you would pay someone else to do what you do throughout the day.

Do you have a business or a hobby? Which do you want? Do you need to make changes?

Notes

Hard Work Works 28

As I was leaving a store one day,
I noticed a T-shirt that a young woman
was wearing.

The back of the shirt said:

Hard Work Works

What more can I say?

28 Notes

Just Do Something 29

There are great resources available on time management.

One common recommendation is to work on those items that will make the most impact on your life. It can be easy to get bogged down in doing little things that are not really that important. Yet, we like to do these little things because they are easy, because they are quick, or we just like doing them. In general, I agree with this advice.

There are times, though, when I just do not feel like doing anything. Can you relate to that?

Sometimes I just do not have the energy or focus for a large project. I have found that it helps to just do something, anything. Once I start doing something, even if it is one of those little things that will not have that big of an impact, it gets me started. Once I get started and build a little

29

momentum, then it becomes easier to get involved in the bigger projects that do matter.

The important concept to remember is that each of us has to discover what works for us. There is no one right way. As long as we get the results we want, then our method is working for us.

Notes

Lessons from *Mary Poppins* 30

Several years ago my husband and I took the grandchildren to see the play *Mary Poppins*. A recurring line was, "Anything can happen if you let it."

This is very true. How often do we keep ourselves from success because we do not let things happen? We do not take risks. We do not open ourselves up to new ideas. We get in our own way. There are many things that we do to not let things happen.

Although I think the line in the play was meant as a reminder to let the good things happen, it can also be a reminder that bad things can also happen if we let them. For example, our health can suffer if we do not eat a healthy diet, if we do not exercise, if we smoke, if we do not manage stress, among many other things. Our professional and personal relationships will suffer if we neglect them. Our career will suffer if we do not continue to improve.

Keep in mind that, "Anything can happen if you let it"—for good or bad. So let the good in and keep the bad out.

30   Notes

Values **31**

Ultimately, values are what define us.

Our values are what make us who we are. It is imperative that we know our values and live by them.

"Actions speak louder than words" applies to values. For example, we may state that we value honesty. However, if we lie to others and to ourselves, what do we really value? It is not honesty.

We need to define our values and then live by them, every day.

31 **Notes**

Who We Are 32

We are who we are because of the choices we have made.

If we like who we are, then we can continue to make the same choices.

If we want to be something other than who we are, then we need to make different choices.

It is that simple... and that difficult.

32 Notes

Do Things that Make You Smile 33

It is said that laughter is good for the soul. I believe this.

I think there are wonderful things that happen to us when we laugh. I think good things happen to us when we smile, too.

When we find something that makes us smile, it makes us feel better, if only for a moment or two. This can lift our spirits and give us a new perspective on the situation we are facing.

I realized this many years ago when I was going through a very difficult time. I happened to glance out the side window as I was driving to work and saw a rabbit sitting by the side of the road. He was just sitting and appeared to be watching the traffic go past. It made me smile.

That was a turning point for me. I knew, in that instant, that I would survive the tough time I was facing.

33

There are many little things that we can do to make us smile every day. Pictures of those we love on our desk can make us smile. Pets can make us smile, and often laugh out loud. A list of accomplishments can make us smile.

What makes you smile? What can you do to set the stage for frequent smiles throughout the day?

Notes

Easer or Jumper? 34

Do you carefully ease yourself into new situations? Or do you jump in?

I am an "easer." I like to ease my way into situations. I like to study the situation, analyze it, develop goals, create a plan, and eventually do something.

I have friends who are "jumpers." Whatever the situation, they just jump into it and start doing things. Sometimes I admire them!

There is no right or wrong. Both methods can get the job done.

A concern with being an easer is that it may take much longer than it should to get results. After a while, more information or planning does not help. However, the result is usually on target.

A concern with being a jumper is that although things are being done, they may not be the right things. Time may

34

be wasted by going back and doing things over. However, at least something is being done.

Which are you, an easer, a jumper, or are you nicely balanced in the middle?

Notes

Persistence or Stubbornness? 35

Persistence is good. Rarely do we reach our professional and personal goals without being persistent.

We need to keep working toward our goals rather than give up. Sometimes, however, persistence crosses into stubbornness. This is not necessarily good.

For example, some time ago I had an evening meeting. I had been to the location before and was certain I knew where it was. It was not there. I drove up and down the road several times without finding it. However, I knew it was there. Finally, I called for directions. The location was farther south than I had thought.

The positive aspect of this was that I was persistent until I found it. The negative aspect was that my stubbornness kept me from finding it sooner. Things are not always as we remember. Sometimes we are wrong. When I arrived, I realized

35

the mistake I had made. I had confused two crossroads.

Be persistent in attaining your goals. However, do not become so stubborn that it holds you back.

Notes

Stop Complaining and Do Something 36

It is human nature to complain.

A certain amount of venting is good. It releases some pressure and stress. It can help us put things in perspective. (Have you ever caught yourself complaining and realized how absurd it could sound to someone who is worse off than you are? I have.)

Complaining can also make us decide to take action and change things.

After a time, however, complaining does not do any good. Alone, it does not fix anything; it does not change anything. It just takes a great deal of our time and energy that could be used for better purposes.

Do you know anyone who has been complaining about the same (probably petty) grievance for years? What a waste!

36

There is a sign that I saw that I really liked. It went something like this: "Pull on your big girl panties and deal with it."

There comes a point in time when additional complaining is senseless. Either take action and do something, or let it go. Put your time and effort into something that will achieve positive results.

Notes

Embrace Yourself While Improving Yourself **37**

It is important that we embrace who we are.

Each of us is unique. We need to appreciate all of our good qualities and accept our areas that need improvement.

At the same time, we need to strive to constantly become better, to improve ourselves. This is a necessary step in achieving professional and personal success.

It is the old saying, "If you always do what you always did, you will always get what you always got."

We may need to improve ourselves by gaining knowledge or technical skills. We may need to improve our interpersonal skills. Whatever it is, we need to become better each day.

It can be difficult to balance embracing who we are with becoming who we want to be. Just remember that who we are today may be perfectly fine for today, but if we want to continue to succeed, we may need to be even better tomorrow.

37 Notes

Use It Or Lose It 38

"Use it or lose it."

I am not sure where this phrase originated, or in what context. It can apply to all aspects of our lives, however.

From a physical standpoint, if we do not exercise our body, we will lose the ability to do the things we take for granted. How many of you have elderly parents or grandparents who could do more if they simply would do more? That will be us someday if we do not continue to use our bodies and our muscles.

From a mental standpoint, we need to continue to use our minds to keep them sharp. Learning new things is a great way to keep your mind young. Studies have shown that learning may also help deter Alzheimer's disease.

We need to continue to utilize our talents to remain skilled. When we do not, we lose the skills we have and will need to regain them.

38

Doing all of these things will help keep us young and active, mentally and physically, as we age.

Notes

The Success We Think We Deserve **39**

Have you seen the movie *The Perks of Being a Wallflower*? There was a line in the movie that still resonates with me: "We accept the love we think we deserve."

I think that we do accept the love that we think we deserve. We accept the treatment from others that we think we deserve. Unfortunately, some of us do not think that we deserve very much.

This concept can also have an impact on our success. We achieve the level of success that we think we deserve, not the level of which we are capable. If we do not think we deserve to be successful, it will be extremely difficult to be successful. People are very good at self-sabotage, and they generally do not even realize it.

I encourage you to think carefully about the level of success you think you deserve. From there, think about why you do not think you deserve a higher level of success. This

39 exercise can give you great insight into those thoughts that may be holding you back.

Notes

Study for A's? 40

I still remember something a high school teacher told my class many years ago. He said that if we study for A's, we may or may not get them.

However, if we study to truly learn and understand the information, the A's will come automatically.

He was right. When I studied to learn the concepts and details of the material, the A's came easily.

I think this concept can apply to our professional lives. If we work to get a raise or promotion, we may or may not get it. However, if we work to truly learn and understand our company and its practices, products, customers, and suppliers, and use this to excel at our jobs, we will find success.

This concept can also apply to our personal lives. If we work to improve our relationships, it may or may not happen. However, if we work to truly understand the people in our

40 relationships and how they think and feel, it will definitely improve our relationships.

What is your goal? To get an "A" or to really learn?

Notes

Stop Studying and Start Doing **41**

If someone would pay me, I could easily be a professional student.

I have always loved school, I think mostly because I love to learn. Even now, I like doing the research for projects and presentations. I like gaining new knowledge and skills.

There comes a time, however, when I need to stop "studying" a topic and start doing something about it.

There are many reasons people do not accomplish what they intend. This is just one. If you are one of those who enjoy the studying and preparation so much that you never finish, it may be time to "leave school" and "enter the real world."

If I can do it, so can you!

41 Notes

Routines 42

Routines help us until they hurt us.

Routines can be very helpful in that they assist us to be productive. They help us be efficient. That is, until something happens and we cannot follow them. We get sick, family members need us, customers want something last minute, and we need to adapt to the disruption of our routine.

Routines can help us immensely. However, we must remain flexible enough that when the routine cannot be followed, we adapt quickly and do what needs to be done.

42 Notes

Business, Hobby, or Required Responsibility? 43

I discussed businesses and hobbies in Chapter 27. Here I will expand on these and discuss a third area, required responsibilities.

We do many things. Most, perhaps all, can be divided into three areas: business, hobby, or required responsibility.

The business area includes everything we do for others that they are willing to pay us to do. If we have a job, we get a paycheck in return for what we do. The work we do has value to our supervisor or the company where we are employed. If we are self-employed, our customers pay us to provide goods or services because these goods and services are valuable to them. In my case, people pay me to speak at their events, and they pay me for my books.

The hobby area includes those things that we do because we enjoy them, but no one is going to pay us to do it. Or they will not pay us very much. Something to keep in mind is, "Businesses are in business to make money. If it does not

43

make money, it is not a business. It is a hobby." (This is the best piece of information I learned at the University of Louisville where I got an MBA.) I love to hike, but no one is going to pay me to go hiking.

Required responsibilities are those things that we are responsible to do for ourselves. This includes everything from feeding ourselves to cleaning our homes to taking care of our pets and/or children. No one will ever pay me to clean my own house; it is my responsibility. And I will never pay someone to clean her own house; that is her responsibility.

With required responsibilities, it is our responsibility to see that they are done. We can do them ourselves, or we can hire someone to do them for us. We can clean our house or hire a house cleaner. We can mow our lawn or hire a lawn service. It does not matter which, as long as it is done.

How would you categorize what you do? Which tasks are business, which are hobbies, and which are required responsibilities?

Notes

Clean House or Change Oil? 44

Previously, I discussed business, hobbies, and required responsibilities.

Required responsibilities are those things that we are responsible to do for ourselves. If we own a business or are self-employed, we have professional required responsibilities as well. These are things that we need to do, but no one is going to pay us directly for them.

For example, we need to have a website, but no one is going to pay us directly for us to have a website. We need to work our costs into our selling price to cover our business expenses.

With required responsibilities, we can either do them ourselves or we can pay someone else to do them. It is my responsibility to clean my house. I have decided not to pay someone else to do it. I am capable of doing it myself, and it does not take that long to do. It is also my responsibility to change the oil in my car. I could learn how to do it, buy the

44

necessary equipment, and determine where to dispose of the oil. I have decided that it is a better use of my time to pay someone else to change the oil.

When I am trying to determine the best use of my time and money related to business, I often ask myself if it is similar to cleaning the house or changing the oil.

Some things, like writing and posting blogs, are similar to cleaning the house for me. I have the capability to do it and can make the time to do it. I also enjoy it. (I enjoy writing; I hate cleaning house. I just want to be clear on that.)

Other things, like designing a website, are similar to changing the oil. I might be able to learn how to do it, but it will never be as good as if a professional did it and it will take me much longer to do it. Also, if I am designing a website, that is time I cannot spend elsewhere. The money I would save doing it myself would probably be small compared to lost revenue. And I would have an inferior website.

In business, we have to decide what we can and should do for ourselves and what we need to hire someone else to do.

Too often I think people see only the business "expense" and try to do it themselves. Many of these expenses are also investments in our business. If we are going to make an investment, it should be the best we can afford. This may mean contracting with someone who can do it better and faster than we can.

What business tasks do you do yourself, and what do you hire someone to do? Should you make any changes?

Notes

Battling Boxes 45

Do you have trouble with people wanting to put you in a box and label it with who they think you should be?

I do. I always have.

I am one of those women who never wanted children. I just did not.

I remember as a very small girl getting a baby doll from my grandma. It was one of the first ones that could be "fed" a bottle of water and in a little while would "wet" its diaper. I dressed it, fed it a bottle, pretended to feed it food, changed the diaper, changed the other clothes because they were wet, and put the doll to bed. I remember thinking, "That was boring!" Yet I could play with other toys for hours.

I hoped that my brothers would have children, because I thought being an aunt would be really cool. (It is.) I also thought being a grandma would be fun, as long as I did not have to go through the mother step first. That worked, too,

45

because it just happened that my husband had children who were almost grown when we married. And being a grandma is fun. And I am still glad I did not go through the mother step first.

When we are very certain about what we want, or do not want, it is important that we stick to that even if family, friends, and society think that they know what is best for us. There are exceptions, of course. We cannot harm others. We cannot expect others to take responsibility for us; we are responsible for ourselves.

If someone is trying to put you in a "box" that does not fit you, say something! Do something! Do not calmly enter the box and let others tape you in and label you.

It is your life. It is your responsibility to decide who you are and live accordingly.

Notes

Be Sensitive, but... 46

**I found this in a fortune cookie:
"Be sensitive, but not overly sensitive."**

I think this is good advice. We do want to be sensitive enough that we are at least aware of how what we do affects others. This improves not only our personal relationships but our professional relationships.

We do not want to be so sensitive, however, that every little word and deed from others negatively affects us. This gives others a great deal of control and power over us. We, not others, need to be in control of our lives and how we feel.

Have you found the sensitivity balance?

46 Notes

Worry, Friend or Foe? 47

I worry too much. I worry that I worry too much!

Worry can get in the way of enjoying life. If we spend time worrying about the future, we cannot enjoy the present. Worry takes time and energy that we could use elsewhere. We can accomplish more if we worry less.

And yet sometimes I wonder if maybe a little bit of worry is good.

If we are a little worried about our future, won't we plan a little better? Won't we do a little more such as get an education, work hard, put money away for emergencies and retirement?

I know that I need to manage my worry. I spend too much time worrying about things that never happen, and are not likely to happen. But I think I will hang on to enough worry that I still feel a need to plan for the future.

47 Notes

Dress to Connect 48

There is always information about how to dress for different situations.

Some of us spend a great deal of time thinking about how we should dress for different professional and personal situations.

One aspect of dress I try to consider is to "dress to connect." What will help me connect with the people around me?

I realized the importance of this many years ago when I was working as a consultant dietitian for a long-term care company. When I went into one of the company's nursing homes it was usually to evaluate the operation of the food service department. To do this I had to be in the kitchen and in the dining rooms. If I was going to be able to do my job well, I had to be comfortable. I also needed to look professional to help gain credibility. I dressed in slacks and a shirt or sweater, flats with a decent sole so I didn't slip, and a lab coat.

48

Many of the consultant nurses I worked with had a different opinion. They dressed in short, tight skirts and high heels. I thought that was rather foolish; how could they work dressed like that?

Something that I did not consider until I overheard some of the facility nurses talking was that the facility nurses did not respect the consultant nurses simply because of the way they dressed. The consultants did not look as though they wanted to actually work; they looked like they just wanted to sit behind a desk and tell others what to do. It was very difficult for the consultants to get the facility nurses to even listen to what needed to be done.

Additional, some of the consultants liked to wear jewelry, big expensive jewelry. The facility nurses interpreted this to mean that the consultants were showing off how much more money they made. It caused resentment, which further eroded the credibility of these consultants. It never would have occurred to me that staff might feel resentment over the jewelry someone else wore, but I can see it now.

I think a good rule of thumb is to dress a level or two above those you will be working with to look professional and gain credibility, but not so far above that you lose respect.

Notes

No Magic Pill 49

Sorry, but there is no magic pill.

There is nothing that we can take that will make us healthy, wealthy, or wise.

There is no magic potion or spell that will give us the life we want.

All we can do is learn everything we can, implement as much as we can, and work as hard as we can for the life we want.

49 Notes

Keep Your Word 50

It is imperative that we keep our word, no matter what.

When we keep our word, people learn that they can trust us. When we do not keep our word, people quickly learn that we cannot be trusted. It can take years to correct that reputation.

We must, of course, keep our promises. The surest way to do this is not to make promises unless we are sure we can keep them. A small promise fulfilled is much more valuable than a large promise unfulfilled. As we keep our promises, people learn that they can trust us.

We must also follow through on our threats. The surest way to do this is never to make a threat unless we are willing and able to carry it out. As soon as we make a threat and then do not carry it out, people learn that they do not need to respect us.

50

Keeping your word applies to both your professional and personal relationships. Stop and think what your employer, employees, customers, and suppliers will think of you if you make promises and do not keep them. It does not take much imagination to see how damaging this will be to you and your success.

The same applies to threats. If you threaten to dismiss an employee, you have to be willing to do so or you send a message to all your employees that they do not need to listen to you. The same applies to suppliers. If you threaten to drop a supplier if certain criteria are not met, you have to move to another supplier if that happens.

Not keeping your word can be just as damaging in personal relationships. What will your spouse/partner, children, relatives, friends, and neighbors think of you if you do not keep your word? Soon you will have taught them that they cannot trust you, that they cannot count on you.

I think the most damage comes when parents do not keep their word with their children. If children cannot trust their parents to keep their promises, whom can they trust? Also, if parents do not carry out their threats, children learn very quickly that there are not any negative consequences to their negative actions. This will not help the child succeed in life.

Before you make a promise, or a threat, determine how you are going to complete it. If you cannot, then do not make it.

Notes

Time Wasters 51

We all have time wasters. We all have things that we like to do that do not give us anything in return.

We cannot succeed if we spend time on these items instead of working.

By time wasters, I do not mean hobbies. We all need to do things to relax, to take our mind off work, to connect with other people, to grow ourselves in ways other than professionally. These things make our life richer.

By time wasters I mean those things that we do that do not contribute to our lives in any way. For example, my time waster is Spider Solitaire. I do not even know why I like it. I do not like computer or video games and do not like games in general. But for some reason I like Spider Solitaire.

So is it a big deal? A game takes only 5-10 minutes. The problem is that those 5-10 minutes could really add up

51 during the course of the day if I let it. That is time spent that cannot be spent on anything else, work or hobby.

What time wasters are stealing time away from your professional or personal pursuits? You cannot succeed by playing Spider Solitaire.

Notes

Equal Partnerships 52

Throughout this book we have talked about *you*. Your rights. Your responsibilities. Your choices. Your life.

It is necessary to remember, though, that everything we have discussed applies to everyone.

This means that if you are in a committed relationship, your partner is just as important as you are. The life he wants is just as important as the life you want. Not more important, but as important.

I think a committed relationship should be an equal partnership. Each person should work equally hard, take on equal responsibility, and give as much support as he or she expects to receive. It is necessary for both people to work together to determine how their life together will meet their individual desires and goals. This might take some negotiating.

The opposite of an equal partnership is a double standard. That is where it is all about one person and about what that

52

one person wants. If you are in a double standard relationship, and it is all about him, can you change things? If not, is it worth staying in the relationship?

If you are in a double standard relationship, and it is all about you, remember that he has the same rights as you do and he can leave you. You might want to make changes before that happens.

An equal partnership is a beautiful relationship. I recommend that you always remember that your partner, and what he wants, is as important as you and what you want.

Notes

Conclusion

Self-empowerment is when you empower yourself to use the power within you to create the life you desire.

An initial step is to think and reflect upon what you do, why, and whether it helps you create the life you want, professionally and personally.

Thinking and reflecting alone are not enough, however. You must take action. Do what you need to do to create the life you want. Only you can do this. No one can do it for you.

An important aspect of self-empowerment is taking responsibility for yourself, your thoughts, your choices, and your actions. Only when you take responsibility do you have power and control over your life.

I hope this book has given you the opportunity to think and reflect upon your decisions and your actions. I wish you the best in your endeavor to empower yourself to create the life you want!

Author's Note

I would like to know what you liked about the book and whether there was anything you did not like about the book. I am constantly trying to improve myself and my work. Your comments, for a second volume of this book and for other books, would be greatly appreciated.

For additional copies of this book, or for copies of my other books, please go to my website, **susanlfarrell.com**. From there you can select your preferred supplier and format (paper copy or eBook).

Thank you, and my best to you in your journey of self-empowerment!

Susan L. Farrell

Acknowledgments

I would like to thank my husband, Rick, for his never-ending support and encouragement. I could not do this without him.

I would like to thank, again, Pat Olson for copyediting and proofreading this book. She did as awesome a job on this one as on the last. I also greatly appreciate her support of my writing.

I would like to thank Sue Gresham for writing the foreword to this book and for being so supportive of the message I want to send to women.

I would like to thank Andrew Welyczko for designing the cover and interior of the book. I am very glad that he agreed to do this for me again.

I would like to thank my parents, brothers, aunts, uncles, cousins, nieces, nephews, and others for the impact they have had on my life. It is said that it is not the destination in life that is important, but the journey. Although this is true, it is the people who share your journey with you who are the most important.

About the Author

Susan has always loved to learn. One BS in college was not enough; she obtained a double major with a minor. Years later, she returned to college for an MBA. Susan also believes deeply in learning everything possible from personal and professional experiences.

Her first career out of college was with a national health care company. She quickly moved from the facility level to division, field, and corporate levels. When she left she had been an executive director with national responsibilities for several years.

As owner of SLF Consulting & Training, LLC, Susan assisted clients with the challenges of combining customer satisfaction, cost control, and regulatory compliance. Her business acumen made her a sought-after speaker which led to a successful speaking career. This, in turn, led to her current writing career on self-empowerment for women.

A normal extension of a love of learning is a love of teaching.

Susan has accomplished this in various positions through teaching and training her employees, co-workers, associates, and customers. She has taught as an adjunct instructor at business colleges. She has informally coached employees, associates, and friends in advancing professionally and personally. She now assists others through her books, blogs, and newsletter.

She is the author of *Don't Act Like Prey! A Woman's Guide to Self-Empowerment,* a book on respectful assertiveness as an option to passive or aggressive behavior. *52 Weeks of Wisdom, A Woman's Guide to Self-Empowerment,* is designed to provide ideas to encourage women to think about what they do, why they do it, and do they want to change. *3 Good Choices: Change It, Accept It, or Leave It; A Woman's Guide to Self-Empowerment* discusses how to make positive choices in all aspects of life.

Susan lives in rural Wisconsin with her husband and three cats.

www.ingramcontent.com/pod-product-compliance
Lightning Source LLC
LaVergne TN
LVHW051503070426
835507LV00022B/2902